contents

what is sleep?

how babies sleep

how much time do
   babies spend sleeping   10
    sleeping needs   12

your sleep versus
   baby's sleep   14

how to work out
   baby's sleep needs   16

where babies sleep
   best and why   18

baby's room and
   baby's bed   20

when baby sleeps
   away from home   22

what is SIDS?
   what you can do to
   reduce the risk   24

establishing a
   bedtime routine   28
    teaching baby to sleep   32

    rocking, patting
    and stroking   36
    singing, reading,
    rhythmic sound   38
    dressing baby in cotton   40
    dummies and comforters   42

daytime sleep hassles   46

getting baby back
   to sleep   48

strategies for
   sleep-deprived parents   52

controversial
   sleep strategies   54
    sedatives   56
    controlled crying   56

lullabies   58

help   60

index   63

We sleep for a third of our lifetime. Most of us take sleep for granted until we have our first child, when suddenly how and when we sleep becomes something we have to plan. The coming of a new baby is such an exciting event that few of us think of asking any advice from experienced parents about what happens after baby arrives. Many parents-to-be think only as far as the birth. When baby arrives home, the parents-to-be are suddenly parents, and many find themselves being pushed along a very steep learning curve!

*There are dozens of myths about how babies sleep and what parents should do. While **Baby Sleep** might contain information which you will find surprising, I am sure there will be something you can use to help you – and your baby – sleep well.*

Viktorija Macens

what is sleep?

Oh Sleep! it is a gentle thing,
Beloved from pole to pole …
Samuel Taylor Coleridge, *Christabel*

There is still much research to be done on the need for sleep and how it works, but we do know that it is as crucial to our health as eating. We also know that there are two distinct phases to sleep, REM (rapid eye movement) and non-REM sleep. The first is the sleep of dreams; the second, non-REM sleep, consists of four phases, each deeper than the one before, and is the sleep which allows the body to re-charge. In adults, periods of REM sleep occur every 90 minutes, in children about every 60 minutes. All of us dream every time we sleep for a long enough period, although we may not always be able to remember our dreams.

> Research has calculated that new parents lose between 400 and 750 hours of sleep in their baby's first year.
> *National Sleep Research Project statistics, published on website: abc.net.au/science/sleep*

how babies sleep

Long before they are born babies have learnt to sleep. Foetal brain waves can be detected at around 20 weeks, and by the time the foetus reaches 30 weeks, patterns of sleep and wakefulness can be determined. We now know that babies dream in the womb. This is because their brains, as well as their bodies, need to exercise in order to develop. At around 25 weeks, a foetus dreams all the time. This gradually diminishes until the baby is born, when she will spend half her sleeping time dreaming.

Newborn babies sleep in REM and non-REM patterns. The first thing new parents need to know and understand about babies and sleep, however, is that babies do not sleep in the same way as adults, or older children, do. Watch your baby as she sleeps. She will grimace, look surprised, smile, move her hands and her whole body. Your baby is dreaming! Then watch your partner, or an older child, sleep – they will be comparatively still. Babies spend more time in REM sleep, when dreams occur, than in non-REM sleep. During REM sleep periods it is easy to wake the child or for the child to wake up on her own. REM sleep gradually decreases as babies grow, until by the time they are three years old, only a third of their time sleeping is spent dreaming. By early adolescence sleeping patterns are the same as an adult's. Not only does dreaming help the brain to develop, but as we age, dreams are also thought to help memory processes. The deep sleep which your baby will grow into at around three months is the most restorative and physically essential type of sleep. Children need deep sleep to grow, and they sleep much more deeply and soundly than adults.

The second thing that new parents need to know is that babies are not born with well-established circadian rhythms, the body's biological cycles of sleeping, eating, activity, resting and waking, which repeat every 24 hours. In fact sleep researchers know now that babies cannot define night from day or active times from quiet times until they are around four months old.

The third thing that new parents need to know is that, as far as parental sanity goes, adults who adjust their routines and expectations to fit in with their roles as new parents have a happier, less stressful time than adults who expect babies to fit in with *their* sleep habits and are unhappy when they don't.

> Premature babies have more REM sleep than full-term babies, possibly because REM sleep helps brains to mature. *National Sleep Research Project statistics, published on website: abc.net.au/science/sleep*

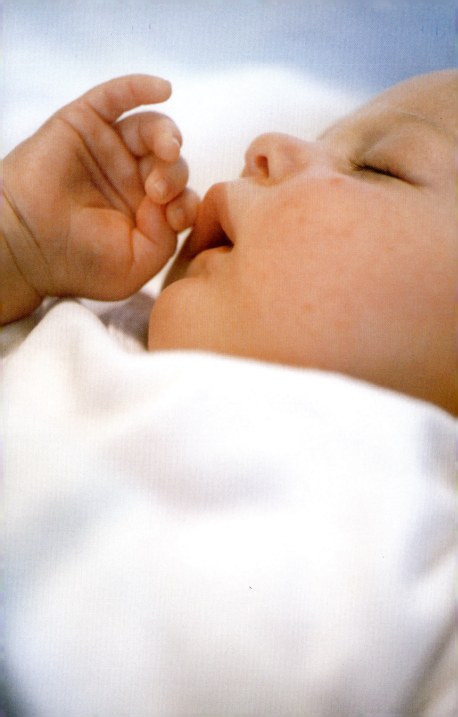

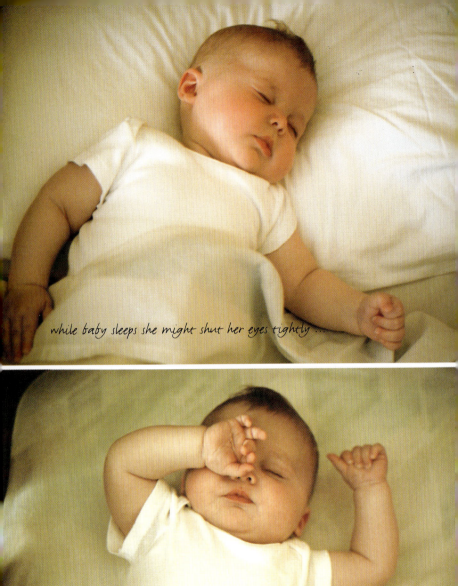

while baby sleeps she might shut her eyes tightly ...

restlessly wave her arms ...

make sucking motions with her mouth …

… then drift into peaceful sleep again

facts about baby sleep

★ Babies' sleep patterns are similar to their feeding patterns – short and frequent.

★ Babies wake more easily than adults, but it is mostly their own bodies which wake them.

★ Sleeping through the night is often a one-off event; the first few times, on average, last for only five hours.

★ On average, babies wake two or three times during the night until they are six months, and once or twice between six and 12 months.

★ Just as babies are individuals when they are awake, so too do they have individual sleeping habits and patterns.

★ Changing to bottle-feeding from breastfeeding, or starting a baby on solids early, will not make him sleep.

Isabella Lettini

★ Sharing your bed with your baby works well for many parents, and provided certain precautions are taken, can be the best way for the whole family to sleep well.

★ Having your baby sleep in your bedroom makes for an easier night's sleep for everyone and decreases the risk of SIDS.

★ You can't make a baby sleep.

how much time do babies spend sleeping?

Every new parent wants an answer to this question which, like the question "How long is a piece of string?", has no one answer. A newborn will have a 90-minute rest-activity cycle, with sleep periods of one to two hours followed by brief periods of wakefulness, both day and night.

Some time between two weeks and eight weeks of age this will begin to move into a 4-hourly cycle. This does *not* mean that baby is ready for the 4-hourly sleep-feed routine made fashionable in the early part of the twentieth century by Dr Truby King. This rigid routine, which is still advocated by some health professionals (and some older friends and relatives), has a poor success record. The vast majority of children will not sleep through the night for the first time until around three months, though it can happen as early as one month and as late as six months of age. One night of sleeping for eight hours, however, does *not* mean that your baby is now sleeping like an adult.

By the time they reach the three-month mark, most babies will be falling into a deep sleep and sleeping for at least one stretch of between six and eight hours in a 24-hour period. Regular daytime sleep periods of between one and two hours are also normal at this age. These will gradually become a morning and an afternoon sleep. Around the age of two years, one in four children will have given up their afternoon nap. Statistics show that babies do not normally sleep for 15 out of 24 hours at three months, despite what some paediatricians may say, and solids do not help them to sleep through the night.

Parents want to know how much sleep a baby "should" have because their baby's sleep patterns are disrupting their own. Parents of newborns may have to wake up and get up every 90 minutes, all through the night – of course they are going to have fragmented sleep.

According to psychologist and sleep expert Stanley Coren, author of *Sleep Thieves*, "Several studies have shown that up to one-third of all parents complain about their children having sleep problems … the vast majority of these complaints turn out to be due to the disturbance that normal childhood sleep habits have caused in the parents' own sleep behaviours."

sleep needs

0 TO 3 MONTHS

Newborns sleep between 16 and 20 hours total a day, for periods of between one-and-a-half hours to five or six hours. Baby's sleep and feeding will be intertwined. About 10 per cent of babies will sleep through for a night (for about eight hours) at four to six weeks of age – this may continue as a regular pattern but in most cases will only occur irregularly.

> Both Dr Spock and Dr Green (well-known childcare authors) advise parents that children will sleep for about 14 hours a day by 12 months – but don't pin your hopes on this figure. It is only an average. Somewhere between nine and 18 hours a day is a more realistic way of looking at it!

3 TO 6 MONTHS

Between three and 12 months, night sleeps of between six and eight hours will become the norm and sleeping 14 or 15 hours in total each day is average. Many babies will wake at least once during this period and may need comforting in order to get back to sleep. Around 12 per cent of parents will find their babies still have a 90-minute sleep cycle.

By three months most babies will be having a sleep in the morning of one to two hours (usually starting around 10am); another short nap in the middle of the day and another one or two hours in the afternoon, beginning around 3 or 4pm.

6 TO 12 MONTHS

By six months about 50 per cent of babies will be sleeping for a six to eight hour stretch at night. About half of these will regress and start waking up again in the next six months, though some will be able to put themselves back to sleep.

If baby is getting around 12 hours sleep a night (not necessarily all in one go), then a one-hour nap in the morning and an early afternoon nap of one to two hours may be enough.

12 TO 24 MONTHS

Morning naps will gradually disappear and baby's afternoon nap may start just after lunch and last for up to three hours.

About one-third of children can stay awake until around 8pm and then settle for the night; many will take another half an hour to settle down to sleep. Try to keep to a routine, even if that means rearranging your own day. Sometimes a walk in the stroller or a ride in the car will put baby to sleep but he will probably wake up when you stop. If you have to go out at night and this disrupts baby's going to sleep, try waiting until he is asleep.

your sleep versus baby's sleep

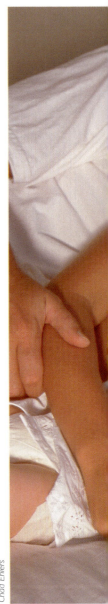

It has been calculated that new parents lose between 400 and 750 hours of sleep in their baby's first year. Broken sleep, though better than no sleep, is not as restorative as unbroken sleep and many parents with children under the age of two walk around feeling like zombies most of the time. In the beginning many new mothers will sensibly adopt sleep patterns which match their baby's. They will catnap during the day when baby sleeps and may in total "get enough sleep" – but because it is fragmented sleep, not deep sleep, they will still feel tired. As baby grows into a toddler parents will continue to suffer from fragmented sleep, and are also likely to reduce the total amount of time they sleep as they resume their pre-baby activities, including returning to a job outside the home.

Fathers today are generally much more involved with the care of their babies and children than their own fathers were. Many fathers do not take enough time off work when a new baby arrives and so are coping with their job while suffering the sleep deprivation that is part of life with their new baby.

Fighting this sleep problem will not make it go away. Unrealistic expectations about how much babies sleep, and about when their lives will "return to normal", can create unnecessary tensions between a couple. Flexibility when it comes to sleep – and to your sex life – is very important in the early days. Accepting that you will have to adopt new sleep patterns is part of the exciting new life you now have as parents – and one of the first lessons in happy parenting.

You'll find a list of sleep strategies for parents on page 54.

how to work out your baby's sleep needs

Sleep charts and diaries are used by sleep clinics to determine how much sleep babies are getting. (You can use them for yourself too.) Filling in a diary will give you a chance to see whether you have unrealistic expectations of how much sleep your baby needs. If you also fill in a diary for yourself (and include all your catnaps) you will be able to see how much sleep you are really getting. If it looks like enough on paper, but you still feel tired, it is most likely that your sleep is so fragmented that you are missing out on deep sleep.

Do this for 10 days and on the 11th day add up the total amount of time the baby has spent asleep, then divide by 10 to get the average number of hours he sleeps daily. You may get a surprise!

Viktorija Macens

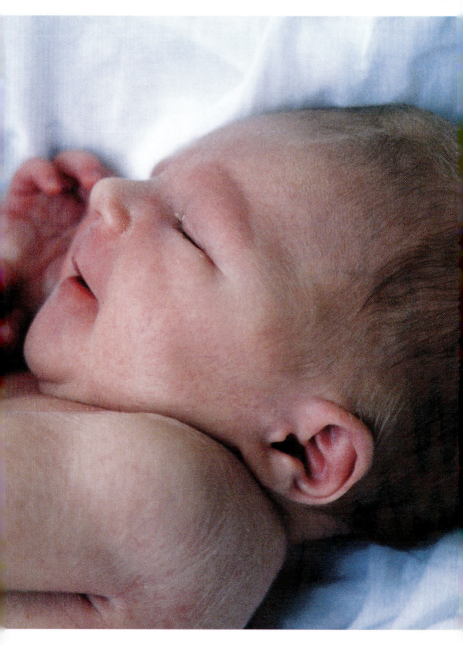

sleep chart

TIME	6AM	7AM	8AM	9AM	10AM	11AM	12 NOON	1PM	2PM	3PM	4PM	5PM
EXAMPLE	M						M				C	C
DAY 1												
DAY 2												
DAY 3												
DAY 4												
DAY 5												
DAY 6												
DAY 7												
DAY 8												
DAY 9												
DAY 10												

M = MEAL OR SNACK   ——— = AWAKE BUT NOT CRYING   C = CRYING   ▦ = ASLEEP

BABY SLEEP

6PM	7PM	8PM	9PM	10PM	11PM	12 MIDNIGHT	1AM	2AM	3AM	4AM	5AM	TOTAL SLEEP FOR 24 HOURS
M	C				M				M	C		

TOTAL HOURS SLEPT (DAYS 1–10)

AVERAGE HOURS SLEPT PER DAY (TOTAL DIVIDED BY 10)

In this example the baby slept from 10am to 12pm (2 hours) plus from 1pm to 4pm (3 hours) plus from 8pm to 11.30pm (3½ hours) plus from 12.30am to 3am (2½ hours) plus from 5am to 6am (1 hour) a total of 12 hours.

SLEEP NEEDS

where babies sleep best and why

For nine months your baby has grown and been nurtured, waking and sleeping, in the warm noisy environment of the womb where he has become familiar with his mother's voice and the sounds of her day, including the voice of her partner. With his birth all this changes – very suddenly. From now on he may be expected to sleep alone, often in isolation. When you think of it this way it is hardly surprising that many babies protest – in the only way they know, by crying. Babies sleep best when they sleep in the same room or the same bed as their parents.

In most non-industrialised societies babies sleep with their mothers. The benefits to the baby of sharing the mother's bed include more stable breathing, less crying, better regulation of body temperature, and a greater likelihood that breastfeeding will be successful. The benefits to the mother include not having to get out of bed to attend to baby, less crying from baby (and perhaps also from mother) and improved breast milk production. And of course both benefit from the closeness of the other.

Babies who sleep in the same room as their parents have been found to have the lowest risk of SIDS; babies who sleep some of the time with their parents in the parents' bed have also been found to have a low risk. Arguments against babies sleeping in the same room – or the same bed – as their parents often hinge on privacy issues, including the notion that the baby's presence will interfere with the parents' sexual activity, an argument which can be easily negated by moving the sleeping baby out of the room during these times.

baby's room and baby's bed

So what about the nursery, you may well ask? It has been said that nurseries are for parents – not babies. This may seem a bit harsh given that there is enormous pleasure for many parents in organising a special room or place for their baby, in planning the colours, buying the furniture and having everything ready for that special day when baby first moves in. The reality is that even if you decide your baby is going to sleep in your room she will still need a place of her own, if only to keep her clothes, toys and other gear for the first few months. You may even decide that you will put her to sleep in this room when the in-laws visit to save answering endless questions about why she isn't sleeping there. It is also true that your baby would be happy sleeping in a box, drawer or laundry basket.

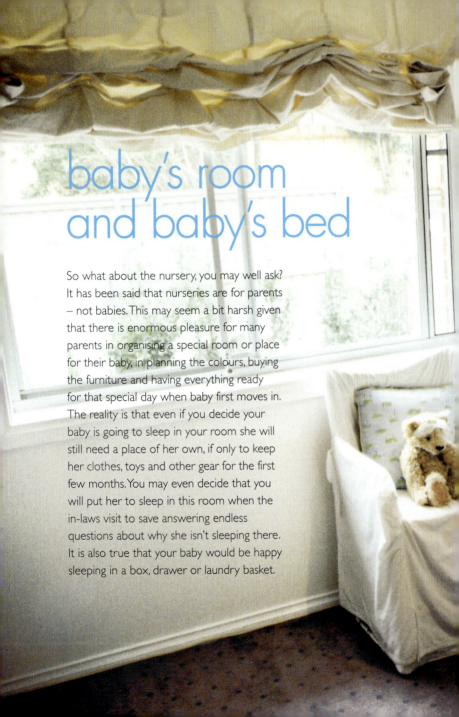

Viktorija Macens

when baby sleeps away from home

In the first six to 12 months you will probably want to take baby with you when you go out to visit other people's houses – at night as well as during the day – at least some of the time. Taking a Moses basket or travelling cot with you, and familiar bedding, will make it easier to settle him. Even so, baby may be unsettled in an unfamiliar environment and you may find that you need to keep him near you – at least up until the age of three months. You may find it difficult to relax if your baby is not settling and sleeping when you would like him to, but the more relaxed you are about the occasion, the easier you will find it and the greater chance you have of enjoying yourself. Once again, flexibility will win the day – though you may find that, with baby-less or judgmental friends, leaving baby home with a baby sitter is the only option.

what is SIDS? what you can do to reduce the risk

SIDS is the acronym for Sudden Infant Death Syndrome (also sometimes called cot death), which is the sudden inexplicable death of a healthy baby. It accounts for the death of more babies aged between one month and one year than any other known cause, so it is of great concern to parents and health professionals. Huge sums of money have been poured into research – you've no doubt heard of Red Nose Day – and there are plenty of theories to be found on possible reasons for these deaths. Research is ongoing into the causes, identifying babies who may be at risk and helping families who suffer these tragedies to adjust.

The National SIDS Council of Australia advises parents to:

★ Always put baby to sleep on his back.

★ Make sure baby's head is uncovered at all times while he is asleep.

★ Keep baby's environment smoke-free at all times.

They further advise parents to make baby's bed so that when he is firmly tucked in, under layers of lightweight blankets, his feet touch the bottom of the bed. A firm, clean mattress which leaves a gap between the mattress and the side of the cot no greater than 25mm is recommended. Waterbeds and bean-bags, quilts, doonas, duvets, pillows, soft toys and bumpers are not recommended.

Other health bodies, such as the National Health and Medical Research Council, advise that it is also all right to put baby to sleep on his side – provided that the arm he is lying on is positioned in front of him in such a way that he is unable to roll onto his tummy.

If baby is sleeping with you, even if it is only occasionally, be sure that you are sleeping on a firm mattress and definitely not a waterbed; that neither you nor your partner smokes at all; that you never take baby into your bed if you have been drinking alcohol or have taken any drugs which induce sleep. Recent research (*British Medical Journal*, July 2000) found that there is no increased risk of SIDS for babies who sleep with their parents when neither parent smokes, whether the baby is returned to his cot or not, especially in babies over the age of 14 weeks. This same study found that there was an increased risk of SIDS for babies who sleep in a separate room, regardless of other risks.

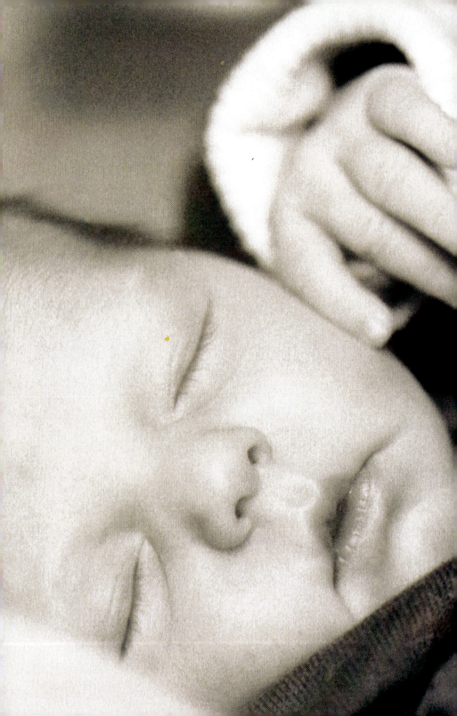

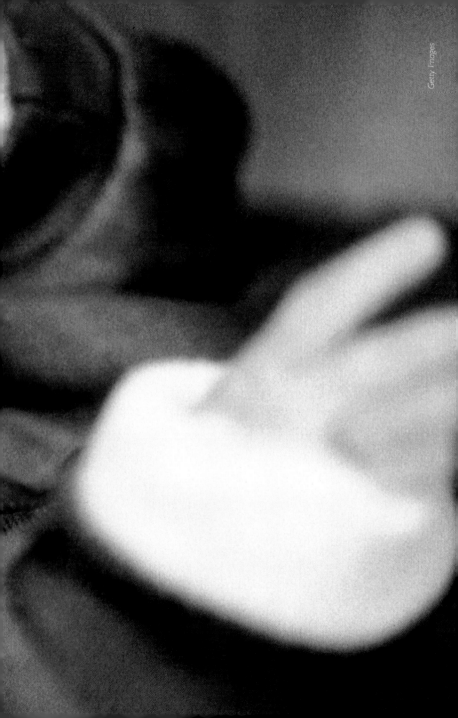
Getty Images

establishing a bedtime routine

In the early days your baby is likely to fall asleep anywhere, anytime, and nearly always at the end of a feed – in fact, whenever it suits him. As you now know you will not be able to make him sleep more – or less – than is his natural inclination. Whether baby is with you in a noisy room with people talking and music playing, or is cradled quietly in your arms in a dimly lit room with music playing softly, he will fall asleep if he is ready.

It is important that you wait until baby is really asleep before you move him – you can tell this has happened when his face is still and his arms fall freely. At this point you can put him gently into his cot or bassinette and with any luck have an hour or two to do other things before he needs your attention, and probably feeding, again. In fact this is a good way to get him used to the idea that his bassinette is for sleeping in.

One thing you don't want baby to get used to is a household which suddenly goes quiet "because he is asleep". This in effect trains him to sleep only in a quiet environment, which as he gets older can make life difficult for you. In large families babies will usually sleep peacefully in the kind of noise that a couple with their first baby would find almost deafening. When a noise or disturbance does wake your new baby it will be because it was unexpected. He is far more likely to be woken by an internal upset, by his legs or arms twitching, by a hunger pang or a sore bottom.

teaching baby to sleep

In the first six months you can start to teach your baby about the difference between daytime and night-time in several ways.

★ Bath him at night before bed – you might like to include a massage as part of this routine.

★ Feed him at night in a quiet, dim place and when he falls asleep put him gently in his bed. During the day feed him in a light, airy room. Make sure you are prepared for having to change or feed him in the night (see Strategies for Sleep-deprived Parents on page 54).

★ Make sure his sleeping place or room is warm – not hot and not cold. Overheating has been identified as a possible risk factor for SIDS and many parents are aware of this. It is easy to be "too careful" about overheating, though – which can mean, in a cold climate, that baby is not warm enough when he is put to sleep, particularly at night. Babies who are not warm enough will wake up. The ideal room temperature for sleeping is 18 to 20°C – all night.

★ Baby should be covered in layers of lightweight blankets, making it easy to adjust the degree of warmth – not thick, heavy covers. As with adults, some babies "sleep warmer" than others. If your baby wakes crying, and you suspect he is cold, test by placing the back of your hand inside his clothing and against his chest. If he feels cold, snuggle him up to you to warm him and when you put him back to sleep add another blanket. If baby is too hot he will sweat, his breathing will become consistently fast, at around 50 breaths per minute, and he will most likely scream.

★ Always go to him when he cries. He is crying because he needs you and if you attend to him immediately he is less likely to work himself into a state of distress and more likely to go back to sleep.

★ Keep night-time for quiet feeds, soothing cuddles and no play, and put him back to bed when he has been fed.

★ Babies sharing their parents' bed or bedroom do not wake any less often than babies who sleep in separate rooms, but they are more easily settled and their night-wakings are less stressful for parents. If you always put baby back to sleep in his own bassinette when he falls asleep (that is, if you are still awake yourself), you will find one night that he has slept for a really good stretch – and so have you.

sleep strategies

When baby won't settle, even after you have fed, changed and cuddled her, and you believe that she *needs* to go to sleep, you can try one or all of these methods, favoured by generations of parents.

swaddling or wrapping tightly

You may have been taught how to do this in hospital. If not, you can ask your Early Childhood Centre nurse or an experienced parent to show you how. With a blanket folded into a large triangle, lay baby down in the middle of the long side. Then, holding one of her arms down, fold the blanket down from one corner and diagonally across her body. Do the same on the other side and you have a little cocoon. (With a tiny baby you can start by folding up the bottom corner.) Some babies find this secure wrapping helps them to sleep, probably because it is reminiscent of the snugness of the womb.

lay baby in the middle of blanket

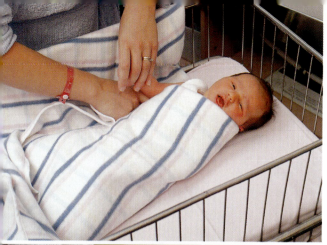

bring one corner of blanket across baby's body, under her free arm and tuck neatly beneath her body

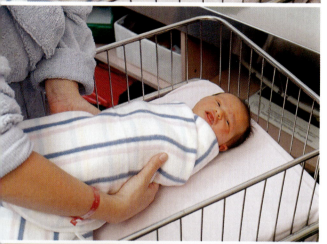

bring second corner across and tuck securely beneath baby's body

tuck end of blanket beneath baby and she will feel securely wrapped

rocking

Rocking your baby as you hold her over your shoulder and gently pat her back soothes many babies to sleep and has the added bonus of bringing up any wind which may be there. If you have a rocking chair you will find it soothing to rock as you feed. If you also hum or sing softly you can continue to sing when the rocking stops and you lay baby down.

Rocking cradles, which used to be the traditional bed for babies and were ideal for soothing them to sleep, are no longer fashionable. Many of the models which replaced them, consisting of a bed which rocked on a frame, are considered unsafe. A more recent alternative is the hammock-style baby bed which comes on a frame that allows gentle, safe rocking.

Your baby sling can also be used to rock baby to sleep. The gentle rocking motion of your walk, so similar to the gentle rocking baby was accustomed to when she was in the womb, will often succeed where other methods have failed.

singing

It is no accident that lullabies are sung in a rhythm which makes for easy rocking. Even if your mother didn't sing lullabies to you, chances are you learnt one or two at preschool. If memory fails you, look for a recording to get you started and to soothe baby as you learn. The rhythms in which lullabies are sung will have the listener (and often the singer) unconsciously adjusting their breathing to a slower rate; their pulse too will slow after 30 minutes.

Traditional favourites include *Rock-a-Bye Baby* (English), *Hush Little Baby* (American), *Sleep Baby Sleep* (German), *Bye Baby Bye* (French), *Maranoa Lullaby* (Aboriginal), *Golden Slumbers*, *Hush-a-Bye Don't You Cry*, Brahms' *Lullaby* and the Mozart lullaby, *Sleep now my little one sleep*. (I have included the words to a number of lullabies on pages 58-59.) You could always make up your own. Choose a gentle rocking melody and make up your own words, using baby's name and lots of references to sleep!

A CD of lullabies is an excellent backup. You may also find that your baby sleeps to music you used to play when you were pregnant (studies have found that newborns will respond to sounds familiar to them in the womb), or to soothing music from classical composers.

reading

You can read to your baby from the very first day. It doesn't really matter what you are reading about, because just the sound of your voice will soothe him; and you can give yourself the opportunity of reading something you needed or wanted to read – be it a congratulations card, the latest Mills and Boon novel or the stock market report.

Getting into the habit of reading to baby is as important as playing with him. There are baby books in strong bright colours with simple pictures, and baby books in black, white and red – any of these will appeal to your baby from very early on. Holding baby as you "read", turning the pages and talking to him is a quiet, comforting activity which can soothe him until he is ready for sleep or actually falls asleep.

> If you have any suspicions about your baby's health, a checkup with your family doctor or paediatrician will set your mind at rest. You can then work on the other strategies listed here. Remember too, that help and advice are always available from your Early Childhood Centre or various local support groups (see page 60). At the very least, you'll discover that other parents are dealing with problems remarkably similar to your own!

patting and stroking

Soothing rhythmical patting or circular stroking, usually on the back, works wonders with some babies. If baby is lying on your shoulder it is easy to pat or stroke in this way. You can also use this strategy when baby is lying on her side in her cot.

rhythmic sound

Sometimes called "white noise", this means a steady rhythmic sound such as that made by a dishwasher, an air conditioner, a clock or a fish-tank filter. Recordings of running water or waves on the sea-shore, or of a mother's heartbeat and the other sounds a baby would have heard in the womb, also work well. Baby's bed can be placed near to the sound source. If you combine the rhythmic sound with swaddling, or rubbing and patting, you may find that this is just what your baby needs.

dressing baby in cotton

Some babies have particularly sensitive skin. If you come from a family with a history of eczema or skin sensitivity you may find that synthetics and woollen fabrics next to your baby's skin are the cause of his discomfort. Of course, you will only know this is the answer when you dress him in cotton and he falls asleep!

Viktorija Macens

dummies and comforters

Some babies need the comforting sensation of sucking more than others. It is your decision whether you offer your baby a dummy or not. It is baby's decision to accept it or not – he may spit it out!

Of the babies who need to suck, some will find their fingers or even a thumb very early on. Some are even born with a blister on their fingers from sucking when they were in the womb.

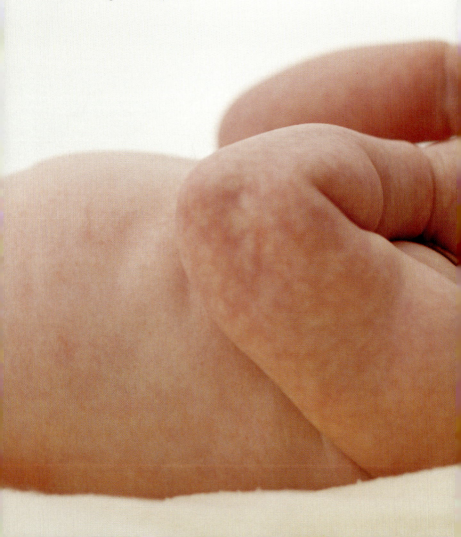

the dummy debate

YES TO DUMMIES	NO TO DUMMIES
Dummies are soothing for babies who like to suck. If a baby who needs to suck is bottle-fed, a dummy is almost essential.	Sucking a dummy is a different action to sucking the nipple, and many mothers who breastfeed prefer not to offer this artificial alternative as it can affect the baby's willingness to breastfeed – breastfeeding requires more effort.
If there seems to be a choice between fingers or dummy, a dummy may be your preference.	Babies who are used to dummies grow into toddlers who like their dummies and sometimes into preschoolers who won't give them up. Dummies can become a battleground.
If the dummy stays in baby's mouth he may start sucking again when he wakes and put himself back to sleep without needing attention.	If the dummy falls out of baby's mouth while he sleeps he may cry when he wakes because it is no longer there. You will need to put it back.
If you are already sterilising bottles and teats, a dummy or two won't make much difference.	Dummies need sterilising – thumbs and nipples don't.
	A dummy in the mouth prevents a baby from using his mouth to explore his world, which is an important part of his development. It also affects his ability to make noises – the beginning of early speech.

daytime sleep hassles

Babies need time awake as well as asleep – from day one they are ready to learn about their new world. They are already familiar with their mother's voice, they know her smell; they may also be familiar with their father's voice. Baby doesn't need fancy playthings and will find her parents the most fascinating thing in her life, and faces – at the right distance – the most fascinating thing of all.

However, some babies, sometimes described as "high needs" babies, need human contact more than others – and all babies need comfort sometimes. For these times a comfortable sling is often the best solution. Finding a sling which allows you to carry baby on your front while she is little, before she has proper head control, which can also be used as a backpack when she is older, is well worth consideration unless you have a back problem. In such cases a baby chair, which can be adjusted to different angles and has carrying handles, is a good second choice.

You can use the baby sling or chair when:

★ Baby needs comforting and you have a task which has to be completed, such as getting dinner.

★ You are shopping alone and you need both hands free.

★ You go for a walk, to a sporting event or on an outing where manoeuvring a stroller is difficult.

Other places babies commonly sleep are car restraints and strollers. The rocking motion of a car is ideal for sending baby to sleep – and many drop off within minutes. It can be tempting to leave baby in a removable car restraint and carry her in it, and for short periods this is unlikely to be a problem. It is important, however, not to confine baby to the curled-up position of the car restraint for any length of time. Strollers are also not recommended as regular beds, particularly for older babies who can roll over, as they can be an entrapment hazard. Leaving baby to sleep occasionally and for short periods in the stroller is unlikely to be a problem, particularly if you check on her regularly. Before baby can hold up her head she needs a stroller which lies back flat and she will naturally fall asleep here at times.

Phillipa Williams

getting baby back to sleep

The first time you mention that you are suffering from sleep deprivation because you have a new baby, you will discover that everyone is an expert! Some will tell you to leave your baby to cry, otherwise "you will become a slave to her whims"; some will suggest "controlled crying", which means the same thing in the end but takes longer (both discussed later). Others will suggest you visit a mother and baby home, try a parent education program or resort to drugs. Still others will suggest you try some of the gentler methods suggested below.

Until a baby is at least 12 weeks old, when she wakes in the night and cries for you it is because she is hungry. Her tummy is small and her digestive system has not yet adapted to taking in enough food to last her for six or eight hours or more. After about 12 weeks she may not be really hungry but her circadian (body) rhythms still have not matured enough to allow her to sleep for long periods, and she will wake needing loving care and possibly needing to suck. Some babies will snuffle or whimper, find a finger or thumb and go back to sleep. Others will need a soothing stroke or pat and others will only be satisfied with a feed.

Viktorija Macens

Viktorija Macens

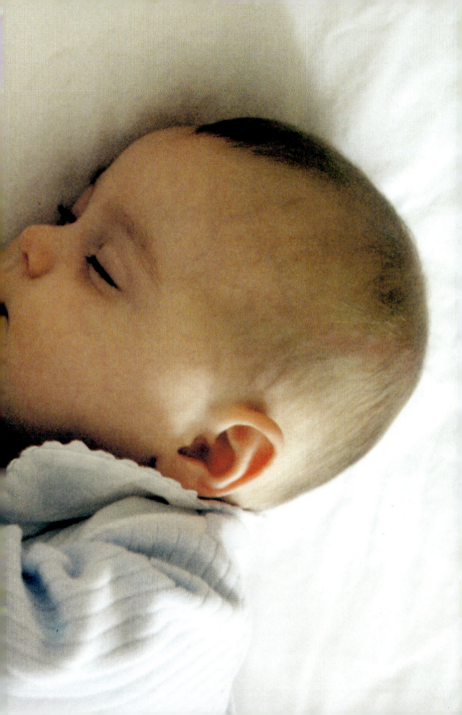

strategies for sleep-deprived parents

- ★ Have baby sleep in your room from the first day home. Remember noise is not an issue for baby – nor is soft bedside lighting. Getting used to the snuffles and noises of a newborn may be more difficult for you, but persevere – it's worth it.

- ★ Experts disagree on whether you should wake baby for a feed before you go to bed, or leave him to wake for a feed when he is ready, in the hope that he will sleep for longer. You will have to decide for yourself which works best.

- ★ Have a set of change clothes (including a bottom sheet) ready – ideally on a foldaway change table – just in case.

- ★ Take it in turns with your partner to get up to baby.

- ★ It is better if you don't have to get out of bed when baby wakes. Reaching over to the bassinette to give him a gentle pat or to rock the bassinette may be enough to help him return to sleep.

- ★ When you need to feed baby, do it in bed. Breastfeeding makes this so much easier as you can place baby in the crook of your arm and nod off as he feeds.

- ★ If baby needs changing, change him after he has emptied the first breast and before he starts the second breast. If he is bottle-fed, stop feeding halfway through the bottle, gently burp him, then change his nappy before giving him the rest.

- ★ When he falls asleep put him back in his cot. If you and baby fall asleep together that's fine – unless you have a waterbed or there is some other possible risk factor for SIDS (see What is SIDS? on page 26).

- ★ When you are feeding baby during the day, make the atmosphere interesting and different. Talk to baby, sing, play. Make sure the room is light and bright. At night, confine your interaction to feeding and soothing – don't talk or play if you want him to take night-time seriously.

controversial sleep strategies

sedatives

Giving a baby a sedative to make him sleep is used as a last resort by some doctors and parents, even though it has been found that babies who are sedated continue to wake at night. Historically babies have been fed everything from gin to opium to make them sleep. These days it is paracetamol, tranquillisers and sometimes old-fashioned gripe water if it is available. If it is tranquillisers, they are often prescribed for the mother as well, when she would be far better off being given supportive practical and emotional help. Before you ask a doctor for sedatives, consider seeking help from a support group, such as a breastfeeding group or baby playgroup, or from your Early Childhood Centre nurse. Try reorganising your life so that you have help with practical things at home and can devote more time to getting your baby's and your own sleeping patterns sorted out.

controlled crying or controlled comforting

This method, sometimes called "extinction" by paediatricians, appeals to a minority of parents, paediatricians and health professionals. It first came to popularity in the early 1950s, spreading from the United States where it was promoted by Dr Spock, the guru of childcare at that time. In the 1980s it was taken up and again made popular by the Australian paediatrician Dr Green. The idea is that the parents are "in control", not the baby – the child is left to cry for a set period, beginning with a short time and building up that time until he falls asleep (often from exhaustion).

There is no denying that this method does work for some families; there is also no denying that it can be an emotionally fraught experience for everyone concerned. In the early weeks and months your baby is crying because he *needs* (not *wants*) attention. He needs feeding, comforting and possibly changing – even if it is the middle of the night!

Health professionals and paediatricians who advocate "controlled crying", or whatever other term they have decided to call this measured approach to comforting, will usually concede that it is not suitable for babies under the age of six months. This is a time when a child has "strong emotions but very little power", as psychologist Penelope Leach (*Your Baby and Child*) says, and no other way of being able to communicate. How does a child of this age let you know that he does not want you to leave the room except by crying? After six months it is said that babies can "learn" that there are times for sleeping and times for waking and that leaving them to cry will gradually teach them the difference. It can also be argued that this method of training older babies and toddlers to sleep when parents dictate is hard on both parent and child and "goes against a mother's basic biology" (Dr William Sears, *The Baby Book*).

There are many sleep programs and books claiming they can teach your baby to sleep. Most of them are the controlled crying method in one form or another. Before you buy or borrow a book, or join a program which promises to "teach" baby to sleep, consider the alternatives — and also the consequences.

★ You need to remember that crying is your baby's only way of communicating with you if you are not in sight or not in the room.

★ When your baby cries you can identify that cry as your baby's own; this is nature's signal to you to comfort him. If you are breastfeeding you may find your milk lets down when you hear his cries — this is perfectly natural.

★ Your baby is learning that he cannot call to you for help. Dr Sears even believes that the baby perhaps "senses that he is a less valuable person" because he can no longer rely on his mother's availability and her ability to comfort him.

★ When you adopt a controlled crying approach you are desensitising yourself.

If you feel you still want to try controlled crying, then be ready to adapt it to suit you own needs and what you know about your baby's personality. Don't feel you have to follow a particular method exactly, or do it just the way your friend did it. If it doesn't work for you, or you simply can't face it, try the methods I suggested on page 54 for sleep-deprived parents.

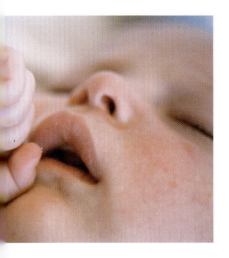

CONTROVERSIAL STRATEGIES

lullabies

Rock-a-bye baby

Rock-a-bye baby, on the tree top,

When the wind blows the cradle will rock;

When the bough breaks the cradle will fall,

And down will come baby, cradle and all.

Sleep, baby, sleep

Sleep, baby, sleep.

Thy father guards the sheep.

Thy mother shakes the dreamland tree

And from it fall sweet dreams for thee.

Sleep baby sleep.

Sleep, baby, sleep.

The large stars are the sheep,

The little ones, the lambs, I guess,

The gentle moon, the shepherdess.

Sleep, baby, sleep.

Hush little baby

Hush little baby, don't say a word,

Mamma's gonna buy you a mocking bird

And if that mocking bird don't sing,

Mamma's gonna buy you a diamond ring.

And if that diamond ring turns to brass

Mamma's gonna buy you a looking-glass.

And if that looking-glass get broke

Mamma's gonna buy you a billy-goat.

And if that billy-goat won't pull

Mamma's gonna buy you a cart and bull.

And if that cart and bull turn over

Mamma's gonna buy you a dog named Rover.

And if that dog named Rover won't bark

Mamma's gonna buy you a horse and cart.

And if that horse and cart fall down

You'll still be the sweetest little baby in town.

Of course if Dad is singing this lullaby, Mamma becomes Poppa!

Hush-a-bye

Hush-a-bye, don't you cry,

Go to sleepy, little baby.

When you wake, you shall have

All the pretty little horses,

Blacks and bays,

Dapples and greys,

Coach and six little horses.

Hush-a-bye, don't you cry

Go to sleepy, little baby.

help

SUPPORT GROUPS

Support groups, where you can talk to parents with babies the same age, can help by giving you the opportunity to talk about what works and doesn't work for you and to hear how other parents cope.

The Playgroup Association has groups – including baby playgroups – in most communities nationally. To find your local playgroup, contact the head office in your state or ask your Early Childhood Centre nurse or at your local council. State phone numbers for The Playgroup Association are:

ACT (02) 6285 4336

NSW (02) 9632 8577

NT (08) 8985 4968

Qld (07) 3371 8253; 1300 362 552

SA (08) 8346 2722; 1800 681 080

Tas (03) 6228 0925

Vic (03) 9388 1599; 1800 811 156

WA (08) 9228 8088

The Nursing Mothers' Association also has support groups in every state. For details on your local group call (03) 9885 0855 or 1300 302 201; fax (03) 9885 0866 or email **nursingm@nmaa.asn.au** to get the number for your state office.

If you think you have a serious sleeping problem you will find Sleep Clinics at many of the major hospitals.

BOOKS

Solving Children's Sleep Problems: A Step-by-step Guide for Parents, by Lyn Quine, Becket Karlson, Huntingdon, UK, 1997
Available only from the Australian Medical Association. Thoroughly discusses all aspects of children's sleep and outlines 29 programs, including "extinction".

Sleep Thieves: An Eye-Opening Exploration into the Science and Mysteries of Sleep, by Stanley Coren, The Free Press, New York, 1996
A book about sleep, with a good chapter on babies' and children's sleep.

The Baby Book: Everything You Need to Know About Your Baby – From Birth to Age Two, by Dr William Sears, Little, Brown & Co., New York, 1993

Your Baby and Child: The Essential Guide for Every Parent, by Penelope Leach, Penguin, Harmondsworth, 1997

The Australian Baby and Child Care Handbook, by Carol Fallows, Penguin, Ringwood, 1998

EARLY CHILDHOOD CENTRES

The **Early Childhood Centres** (run by local councils) referred to in this book are known by this name in New South Wales – in other states such centres may go under other names such as Child Health Clinic, or even Maternal and Child Health Clinic. Contact your local council for help.

index

afternoon nap *10, 12, 13*
alcohol *27*
baby backpack *48*
baby chair *48*
baby sling *36, 48*
bean-bags *27*
bedtime routine *7*
blankets *7*
bottle-feeding *7*
brain waves *7*
breastfeeding *8, 20, 44, 54, 57*
broken sleep *14*
car restraints *48*
catnapping *14, 16*
circadian rhythms *4, 50*
controlled crying *56-57*
cot death *26*
cradles *36*
crying *34, 50*
daytime sleep *48*
deep sleep *4*
dreaming *3, 4*
dressing in cotton *40*
dummies and comforters *42-44*
eczema *40*
flexibility *24*
4-hour sleep-feed routine *10*
Green, Dr *56*

grimacing *4, 6*
gripe water *56*
high needs babies *48*
"Hush-a-bye" *59*
"Hush little baby" *59*
King, Dr Truby *10*
lullabies *38, 58–59*
massage *34*
mattress *27*
morning nap *10, 12, 13*
Moses basket *24*
naps *10*
newborn sleep needs *10, 12*
noise and sleep *32, 54*
non-REM sleep *3*
nursery *22*
overheating *34*
paracetamol *56*
parental expectations *4*
parental sleep deprivation *50, 54, 56-57*
patting and stroking *40*
premature babies *4*
privacy *2*
reading *38*
Red Nose Day *26*
REM sleep *3*
  in premature babies *4*

rhythmic sound *40*
"Rock-a-bye baby" *58*
rocking *36*
sedatives *56*
sex life *14, 20*
sharing your bed *8*
SIDS *8, 20, 26, 34, 54*
6 to 12 month sleep needs *13*
"Sleep, baby, sleep" *58*
sleep chart *18-19*
sleep deprivation *14*
sleep-inducing drugs *27*
sleep needs *12-19*
sleep routine *13, 30*
sleep strategies *36-40*
  dressing in cotton *40*
  dummies and comforters *42-44*
  patting and stroking *40*
  reading *38*
rhythmic sound *40*
  rocking *36*
  singing *38*
  swaddling *34-35*
  white noise *38*
sleeping through the night *8, 10*
solids *8, 10*
Spock, Dr *56*

storing baby's equipment *22*
strategies for sleep-deprived parents *54*
strollers *48*
Sudden Infant Death Syndrome *26*
swaddling *38-39*
baby bed *36*
synthetic fabrics *40*
3 to 6 month sleep needs *12*
tranquillisers *56*
travelling cot *24*
12 to 24 month sleep needs *13*
waking *8, 50*
waterbeds *27*
white noise *38*
woollen fabrics *40*

Editor-in-chief Mary Coleman
Managing editor Susan Tomnay
Senior editor Georgina Bitcon
Editor Anne Savage
Design concept Michele Withers
Designer Mary Keep
Photographer Scott Cameron
Stylist Mary-Anne Danaher
Illustrator Jo McComiskey
Sales manager Jennifer McDonald
Group publisher Jill Baker
Publisher Sue Wannan
Chief executive officer John Alexander

Produced by *The Australian Women's Weekly* Home Library, Sydney.

Colour separations by
ACP Colour Graphics Pty Ltd, Sydney.
Printing by Dai Nippon Printing, Hong Kong

Published by ACP Publishing Pty Limited,
54 Park St, Sydney; GPO Box 4088, Sydney,
NSW 1028. Ph: (02) 9282 8618
Fax: (02) 9267 9438.

awwhomelib@acp.com.au
www.awwbooks.com.au

Australia Distributed by Network Distribution Company, GPO Box 4088, Sydney, NSW 1028.
Ph: (02) 9282 8777 Fax: (02) 9264 3278.

United Kingdom Distributed by Australian Consolidated Press (UK), Moulton Park Business Centre, Red House Road, Moulton Park, Northampton, NN3 6AQ. Ph: (01604) 497 531 Fax: (01604) 497 533 Acpukltd@aol.com

Canada Distributed by Whitecap Books Ltd, 351 Lynn Ave, North Vancouver, BC, V7J 2C4, Ph: (604) 980 9852.

New Zealand Distributed by Netlink Distribution Company, Level 4, 23 Hargreaves St, College Hill, Auckland 1, Ph: (9) 302 7616.

South Africa Distributed by PSD Promotions (Pty) Ltd, PO Box 1175, Isando 1600, SA,
Ph: (011) 392 6065.
CNA Limited, Newsstand Division, PO Box 10799, Johannesburg 2000. Ph: (011) 491 7500.

Fallows, Carol.

Baby sleep.

Includes index.
ISBN 1 86396 223 9.

1. Infants – Sleep. 2. Infants – Care. I. Title.
(Series: Australian Women's Weekly
parenting guides; 3).
649.122

© ACP Publishing Pty Limited 2001
ACN 053 273 546
ABN 18 053 273 546

This publication is copyright. No part of it may be reproduced or transmitted in any form without the written permission of the publishers.

Cover photograph Viktorija Macens
Back cover photograph Isabella Lettini

The publishers would like to thank the following for help in preparing this book:

Sudden Infant Death Association (SIDS), NSW, Australia, phone (02) 9681 4500

Royal North Shore Hospital, NSW, Australia

Products used in photographs were supplied by:

Avent products, NSW, Australia,
phone (02) 9436 0723

the baby's ark, NSW, Australia
phone (02) 9326 5036

Baby Bjorn, Vic, Australia,
phone (03) 9645 0222

Britax Child-Care Products Pty Ltd, Vic, Australia,
phone (03) 9288 7288.